# Wheel of Life

# Wheel of Life

Rama Gupta

STERLING

**STERLING PUBLISHERS (P) LTD.**
Regd. Office: A1/256 Safdarjung Enclave,
New Delhi-110029. Cin: U22110DL1964PTC211907
Phone: +91 82877 98380
e-mail: mail@sterlingpublishers.in
www.sterlingpublishers.in

*Wheel of Life*
© 2020, Rama Gupta
ISBN 978 81 947772 6 7

All rights are reserved.
No part of this publication may be reproduced, stored in a retrieval system or transmitted, in any form or by any means, mechanical, photocopying, recording or otherwise, without prior written permission of the original publisher.

Printed in India

*Printed and Published by* Sterling Publishers Pvt. Ltd.,
Plot No. 13, Ecotech-III, Greater Noida - 201306,
Uttar Pradesh, India

**This anthology of poems is**
*dedicated to*
**DAISAKU IKEDA,**
**my mentor**
whose guidance has been a constant source of inspiration for my poems.

# Acknowledgements

I would like to first acknowledge gratitude to Dr Rana Nayar for his detailed comments and valuable suggestions that I found a never failing source of illumination. I am immensely grateful to Sh B D Kalia who provided me advice and encouragement when it was most needed. I am thankful to Dr Kailash Chander Ahluwalia without whose wisdom and sincere advice I would have given up long-time back. I wish to thank my husband Col DP Gupta, who helped me throughout the project providing steady support, suggestions and endless corrections. Lastly, I would like to thank my daughters Vandana, Neelam and my son Amit not only for assisting with editing my work but also for their candid opinions and unwavering faith in me and my writing.

# Author's Note

On my retirement, the apparent stability of my day to day life was unexpectedly interrupted.
This caught me completely off guard, and I went through a phase of existential crisis, full of insecurity, fear and confusion. At that time, I visited my daughter in Sydney, Australia. One day my son-in-law took me to New castle, where I was so captivated by the immensity of the ocean, that I wrote a poem on the spot. I realised for the first time that every aspect of manifest reality is in a state of constant flux. Everything is changing all the time and nothing that exists is permanent. That fearful knowledge, that one day, one's eyes will no longer look out on the world, dawned upon me. One will no longer be present at the universal morning roll call. The light will rise for others, but not for me. There will be new visitors on the shore but I will not see them.

Writing poems brings a reconciliation between oneself and all of one's pain and fears. This book is that reconciliation for me. I hope you are able to feel a similar emotion too, on reading my poems.

# Contents

| | |
|---|---|
| *Acknowledgements* | *vi* |
| *Author's Note* | *vii* |
| 1. A letter from home | 1 |
| 2. A paleolithical goddess | 2 |
| 3. A spiritual seeker | 3 |
| 4. A weird journey | 4 |
| 5. Ah human life | 7 |
| 6. At the Pond's lake | 8 |
| 7. Clouds | 9 |
| 8. Darkest night in Panchkula | 11 |
| 9. Do not worry about death | 13 |
| 10. Dwarka | 15 |
| 11. Foetus killing | 17 |
| 12. Galileo Galileo | 19 |
| 13. Love in a digital age | 21 |
| 14. Grand Canyon | 23 |
| 15. Growing old gracefully | 25 |
| 16. Happiness | 26 |
| 17. Higher consciousness | 28 |
| 18. Hot springs of Tattapani | 30 |
| 19. How do we know what we want? | 32 |
| 20. Lord of my life | 34 |
| 21. I am not a saint | 35 |
| 22. I ask myself | 36 |
| 23. I awoke before the sunrise | 38 |
| 24. I never thought her memories would hurt her | 40 |
| 25. After the break-up I ran to the woods | 42 |
| 26. If God comes | 44 |
| 27. Innocence of a child | 45 |
| 28. It happens once | 47 |

| | |
|---|---|
| 29. The lord loves you | 48 |
| 30. Landscape | 49 |
| 31. Live in - Relationship | 51 |
| 32. Losing someone | 53 |
| 33. Love her | 56 |
| 34. Morning mountains range beyond Simla town | 59 |
| 35. River | 61 |
| 36. My Other self | 64 |
| 37. New castle | 65 |
| 38. Night | 66 |
| 39. Oh lord I know one thing | 68 |
| 40. Old people's home | 70 |
| 41. One needs a teller | 71 |
| 42. At the Pond's lake | 72 |
| 43. Walk on snowy evening | 73 |
| 44. Stop by my house | 75 |
| 45. Prayer | 77 |
| 46. Sanctum sanctorum | 79 |
| 47. Spring has come | 81 |
| 48. The black birds | 83 |
| 49. The cycle rickshaw puller | 85 |
| 50. The sunsets | 87 |
| 51. Veiling divinity | 89 |
| 52. Walk with my grandchild | 91 |
| 53. Walk the dog in fifth avenue | 93 |
| 54. What deodars do for human spirit | 95 |
| 55. Who am I Part-I | 97 |
| 56. Who am I Part-II | 99 |

# A letter from home

She tells me stories of life,
Of the familiar Simla hills,
Autumn dusk, cloudy sky,
Frost at midnight.
She writes:
The apples are gathered and packed
Ready to send.
She gives me news
Of what happened in my absence?
Tenderly tells story of her loneliness and loss.
Much more and many more
Finer shades of feelings,
I could read.
Then she communicates.
Excited
How Anu climbs and runs around.
She tells me of her pain.
It flares up like fire,
Blisters me too.
The things we experience,
When we are alone
Are much stronger and fresh .
My life here on remote mountain
Is harsh and hard
Still
I smilingly read
With excitement her plans:
How we would live our life when alone.
But know that it never happens
What we soldiers plan.
Life is strange and harsh,
I hear the music of the autumn
I reach down to pick up her envelop
The rose petals fall,
Smell of home.
I gaze at the same sun
Blazing up the Pir Panjjal ranges
Above my bunker
As on Simla hills.

# A paleolithical goddess

I crawled through the cave
Though knee deep in cold water for long time
Invoking her.
It has nothing on the walls.
Silence is grafted here like the wilding.
It is dark and cold.
They say sinners won't reach her.
The Great mother has no face
How can mortal sculpt that divine face?
What for does it need a body?
She is energy incarnate.
Which body can sustain that flow of energy?
Great mother's visage is her bulging belly
Great mother has no feet.
What for does she need her feet?
Where is she to go?
Devotees come seeking her favours here.
Will no voice of God or demon or mortal tell me
Why they surrender to higher power?
Is it they feel the pure awareness of their existence
That gives a human being, real strength.
Or is it their human need
To serve the energy
To obey that energy,
To attend to it,
To be nourished by it,
Rather than to manifest
That energy in action and understanding.
She is silent the way the deepest water is silent.
Her eyes are two hollow - pools
To swim away from the world to love and heaven.

# A spiritual seeker

A spiritual seeker
chanting fervently
In ringing voice
In sunshine and in shadow,
Journeyed long
In search of Buddha land.
But he grew old-and tired
fell
As he found no spot
That looked like Buddha land.
His strength was failing
When he felt a shadow on his body
He asked "Shadow,
Where can it be-
This land of Buddhahood?"
"Over the Mountains
Of the Moon,
Down the Valley of the Heart.
Forge ahead,
Gallantly, vigorously
Make ceaseless efforts
If you seek Buddha land
This perilous journey inward is hard and slippery."
The shadow replied.

# A weird journey

When your spouse is threatened
With serious illness,
You are scared.
Life becomes a weird journey into fear.
You do not probe this enigma,
That you dread.
Nor do you want to find the answer
To existential perplexities
But you continue to fear.
Like any contemporary woman
I was busy with my own pursuits:
Economic independence, privacy,
And personal space.
Believing: No one is that starry eyed anymore.
Emotional intensity,
In an era of intrusive technology,
Is scary, not desirable at all.
All consuming relationship is not possible any more.
Why is he the centre of my existence now?
I have eyes only for him,
I see him through closed eyes,
Hear his sound of pain coming from closed mouth.
When there is slight change in his posture
My heart does a couple
Of hops, skips and jumps.
The mind switches on automatic mode
Relaying all the scenes
Of his undiagnosed illness.
And unwittingly creating terror
Carrying it to bed.
Nightmares don't leave a moment of rest.
Fear with an extended arm
Drums up the beating of the heart
The things I have dreaded thinking,
I imagine happening to him.
Fear grips completely

Shuts me as a captive
Within its four walls,
Darkness wraps like a shawl
Which I can't remove
Even while having a shower.
It stays in the backdrop,
While life presents different scenes
I wake up in the middle of night
Putting hands before his nostrils,
Making sure he is breathing
Slight throat irritation or cough
Is a sign that points to terrible disease?
I do not want to know
Or I don't want to say
Its name I want to avoid.
His release of an arm from under the head
Or any turn, puts me on alert.
Mind,
A masterful weaver of whimsical, intensely terrible stories,
Makes me suffer silently.
I pretend to sleep,
But waking self sees
What procedures he would undergo the next day.
Life goes in measuring doses
And asking and answering queries.
His illness has brought the rest of my life to a standstill
It has created a terror zone of its own.

Whenever the nurse calls
I run with the trepidation of
Not seeing him anymore.
Why this vulnerability
Why no need for privacy
Why space and identity
Are no more sacrosanct?
Love should nurture freedom not stifle it.
But now the space throws up
More stress and chaos
Rather, I want some sound to keep me company
May be phantoms of air,
Echoes of the night,
Or the sweeping shapes of clouds,

The howling of dogs
In the distance
I do not mind the darkness of the dawn
Or the dread of the night,
Even the early temple bells
For that matter
Any rituals or morning services
I am not a religious person
But at least
These routines hold you in place.
How I wish to inherit hope,
And the gift of forgetting,
To erase it
From the darkest corners of my mind.
Let hope come if we've got to go on living.

# Ah human life

Ah human life is a harsh cord
That binds us, wounds us;
While leaving
Covers us like sheets
All you loved of her lies here.
Only the wind blows out
Where does the self actually go?
All the accumulation of memories that threads life together:
All the love, laughter or loss
And where does it all go
When someone dies?
The kinsmen and all others who hold us dear
Come in white-robed forms,
Given in agony
Burying us,
Crowned with lilies and roses,
In the darkness of the grave
And know not where or unto whom we go.
They cannot follow me, says the soul
Look, how empty we go through the world
Without ears, without eyes, without touch,
Without air, without sound, without substance
The traveller,
Travelling through it,
Dare not openly view it .
The spirit walks in shadow
Its mysteries are never exposed
To the weak human eye.
And bore us away
By a route obscure and lonely,
To shut us up in a sepulchre
In this kingdom by the sea
Or with a dumb stone on the earth.

## At the Pond's lake

Every morning I walk swiftly
With forward glances to The Pond's lake.
The waters have settled after the night of rain.
I do not dip the cupped hands in the lake
I feel cold in body.
Though the sun is moving along the landscape,
The billowing trees, thick with blossoms glistening,
The centipedes emerging from wet earth
Shaking in the wind.
The pathways circle around the shining lake
The black ducks float on cold water,
A strange bird fluttered alone in the sky
A duck swimming in the sunlight saw it

In the meantime another took a vertical flight
Whistling something sweet
Of connectedness, of recognition
That we share the same land
Is it not beautiful? It said

Yes, such moments of silences and stillness
Amplify the existential kinship
At once I feel one in the family of things
No stranger or visitor anymore.

# Clouds

I was running with joy on the Jakhu hill
Afternoon of peculiar splendour,
Earth and air conspiring in beauty.
It was just as the light was beginning to fail.
Suddenly I saw -all I needed to see –
Clouds,
In the darkening mountain's side
Lightly and slowly travelling over the sky,
Sometimes drawing their veils and then spreading it wide.
Now standing firmly like a vision fled.
Is this the poetics of nature?
Its colours and emotions
they are celebrating
In this language of sky.
I wonder

How they forever find some new play.
I saw them down on hands and knees
Busy with hiding moon,
Her shadowy beams,
I found their arms full of it
That harm should not come of it;
So built the screen
And gave these stars back their shade
To prove they cared.

Anyway the delicious pleasure is to watch them appear
As they rise and create:
Shapes here, there formless masses of the hour;
Here lions I was watching , there elephants appeared
Then like soldiers ,
Dressed in silvery robes,
Wide white caps ,
Arrayed in marching order;
An army moves.
Higher and higher it ascends.
Some scatter and fall

Others soar in air
As if impelled by some celestial call.
Triumph is the noblest impulse of the soul!

They seemed to swell and swell,
Their bulbous eyes became radiant.
Their faces grew huger and huger,
All the time until I thought,
They would blot the universe.

These systematic succession
Of the forms of the unlimited,
Infinite, the sublime
Something impersonal,
Universal.
I cried with joy and tears
Shouted 'Hallelujah'
Into the solitary cell of the mountain air:
The mute plea -the plea of life facing beauty.
 Who thought it all, created it all
The more they expand,
The more layered and beautiful
The symphony of the spirit became
Almost blessedness.

Their magic enchants me
To have longing for transcendence
And elevate human life.
More than once I wished to be them.
All the soul's secret thoughts
Seem to move towards
The animating and creative
Principle of the whole world:
That life itself is cloud,
Living, moving, fleshy, substantial and corporeal.
Won't they which today have risen to heaven
Tomorrow,
By the world's attraction
Be driven downward
To sink in drops
And rest in Mother Earth's breast?
There in an inherent balance to life -
 that what we give will soon be replenished.

# 8

# Darkest night in Panchkula

Where was it written that I would go to the window?
The warm air of the summer would be filling the trees with the odour of grass
Suddenly the swirling dark clouds of tear gas would rise in Panchkula
The followers of Ram Rahim sect,
Fleeing towards this dividing road of sector two and four.
Tonight of all the nights,
A man running would catch his breath,
Lift his head, look back ward in the slant of light,
Loosed a bellow that broke and rolled like thunder in the air.
A stranger appearing from nowhere would rip open his belly with his bullet,
Making his moment in front of my house his last.
Where was it written that their world of faith would fall apart?
Making room for the sight of the god man
Chained and pronounced as rapist,
Driven to jail.
Have they found their angel or uncovered this demon?
In spite of the swiftness with which the catastrophe approached,
Tempestuous emotional climates swept over them unpredictably.
Then something shifted,
All these devotees,
Driven by faith,
Wishing the glimpse of their saviour
With seething inner turmoil
Fleeing the scene
Created ruckus:
Scaling the walls
Smashing the windows and cars
Media vehicles and whatever came their way.
Who could replace that awful sight,
Of fire, bullets and blood?
Many neighbours
Gathered behind the locked door and window
They saw them falling like flies,

Their dark bodies, sinking into wounds
Becoming the infinitesimal part of that dark night
Where the shattering of the dreams,
The ruin of the stars enjoy the same fate.
Where was it written?
Here would spread the night
Darkly inscribing the scars everywhere on everyone
And I would be standing by the window
Watching flesh falling
Soundlessly, swiftly into the abyss of the night
The time seeming like an eternity.

# Do not worry about death

Do not worry about death
If it comes like a swine flu or a road accident,
Thrusting me with enormous force,
Rendering me unconscious
Or slipping me in and out of consciousness.
I will step through the dark door
With that sweet feeling
People have
that let themselves slide into sleep.
If it comes as cancer, a deadly disease
I will neither wince nor cry aloud.
Even in its clasp
I would bravely fight it
Standing my ground.
Till one day there is less to do
With the commodities of life
And more to do with the waiting
For appointments, tests and procedures.
Won't death be then the easy exchange
Or say freedom from all troubles?
In case, death is sudden and violent
Strikes in most wanton time of my life
I won't have time to stare into its face
You are gone before it gets there.
Why worry about the shortness of life
When there are no longs,
No shorts to things
That are no more.
Long life, say of even Methuselah
Or short life of lily of a day,
Both are by death made all one.
It is also a possibility,
Death comes showing a friendly face,
Just as philosophers promise.
You die in the same way as you fall asleep-
By drifting away

Hearing other people's voices
On the edge of the soul,
Gliding and drifting, losing much of its fear.
Whatever way the life ends,
The death shall find me unafraid.
Why complain of the same destiny,
That involves everyone
Moreover,
Whenever your life ends,
It is not all over still ,
It is a certainty :
There is life before and after
I consider Eternity another possibility.
Not yesterday I learnt
If you fear death while you are alive
It is dying all the while you live.
Is it not enough to understand
There is still nothing like living?
Now I love the world more
Because it is transient
I pay generous and living attention
Asking no questions.
Just surrendering
To life's unknowable and uncontrollable, unfolding graces.
I want to end up touching many lives
Or filling mine with more aliveness.
And go with serenity and courage
Not even mixed with the grief of passing.

## 10

# Dwarka

There were temples or there were none
On an island
Or only Dwarakadheesh temple -
The original temple built by
Krishna's grandson,
Vajranabha, over the Hari-Griha
Lord Krishna's residential place
As they say

Did an ocean swallow it or it didn't?
Was there any one to witness it?
Did they have someone to fight?
This happened or it did not.
A beautiful city of Dwarka stood there
On the banks of river Gomti
As old as Mahabharata epic
With the temple of Dwarkadeesh-
King of Dwarka-
Or so we think.

They were meant to stand for ever
They were consecrated,
God- centric
Primal, pristine.
Never extracted from air, fire, water or earth
We suppose.
For the generations to see
Sri Krishna lived here
A deadly arrow shot
From killer hunter
Jara perhaps by mistake
On Sri Krishna's toe.
Krishna never hesitated
To leave like before
His gopis, kingdom and now even his life,
Being ever fixed in witness - self,

Demonstrating,
The cosmic union with the Absolute.

A meteor fell or volcano erupted
Or was it the coastal erosion
That destroyed it all
Or with the going of Krishna
The Dwaparyug disappeared
So did Dwarka.
Someone summoned something
Or it manifested in new form
More or less this Dwarka
Five-storey structure
With seventy-two pillars
And spire 78.3m high.
Part of the Char Dham pilgrimage
The other three being
 Rameswaram, Badrinath and Puri.
A gateway to heaven
They think.

## Foetus killing

What shall I tell you?
The child I conceived but did not get.
Abortion will not let me forget
The wet small pulp with no hair that you were, my child,
That did not breathe the fresh air
Nor see the ray of day light.
I have stolen your birth, your name and your games
I haven silenced your giggles, baby tears.
I stifled your love, your marriage, your dreams
 Your plans for the future:
A doctor or an astronaut or a singer you could have been.
Young, angelic, adorable girl
I hear your cries in the voice of the winds
That runs like a mad thing into the night.

May a mother never hear these stirrings of the soul
May she never feel the tears
Falling like fat rain,
And wet the breast that you did not suck.
I seized your fortune before you could live that lovely life.
And all the little people
Stare at me and say,
"That is the Crazy Woman
Who killed her girl child at night?
Your oak-eyed mother did nothing
Nor change her bloody gaze
As Death sprawls on the bloody floor of the bedroom
Peers at her love's departure through the bedroom door.

Yes I feel guilty that I poisoned your beginnings
I whine but was the fault entirely mine?
Yes, you were born
You had body
But you died before time.
You are dead
Neither grief nor love is enough to ratify it

Is the fault entirely mine?
What can I say?
How the truth is to be told?
One thing I know
You did not giggle nor cried
But you died

Believe me my child I love you
Believe me I know you,
I love you
I love you.
Nothing can make me forget you.

## Galileo Galileo

Rome is the land of Galileo,
The city in which he was tried.
Galileo- the Italian polymath
Worn by a long life of scientific research,
Found in the Book of Nature
Truths not stated in the Book of God.
Holy Church denounced him
Forgetting that the Book of Nature is also a Book of God.

He didn't hold up these religious despots in reproach.
He was most surprised at the fear of these men.
Questions rose in his mind:
Why cannot a man act himself,
Be himself, and think for himself?
Can the study of truth, do harm?
Doesn't every true scientist seek only to know the truth?
Shall we dread the search for it?

It seems to him that naturalness alone is power;
Hunger of the mind asks for knowledge of all that is around.
Genius only lights the way for him like a distant sun.
As his lifetime unfolded
He grew only more insistent on truth over illusion
And let us have truth, he felt,
Even if the truth be the awful denial of the good God or religion.
We must face the light,
Not bury our heads in the sands.
He pushed on and on,
Revealed new ways in which God works,
and brought to us deeper revelations of the wholly unknown.
Every formula which expresses a law of nature
Is a hymn of praise to God
He thought.
He grew old
Weak and feeble,

Trembling before that tribunal-terror impersonate
Declared that to be false
Which he knew to be true.
It was not that he found
Religion's promises of immortality
Alluring as he confronted his own mortality.
Rather religion was used to justify injustice
Those who followed him were convinced
The blood of the martyr is the seed of truth.

# Love in a digital age

I know of a girl, fair and young,
Who fell in love
At the click of the button.
She meets
She texts
She asks
She gets the answers
She chats till 2 am.
What a bliss!
The digital world provides
Lovers with the armour
For instant gratification.
Technology and apps are all facilitators
There are no impediments to their union
Now date is a click away,
A love interest is a text away.
What joy she revels in
What an amiable peace!
Then it is all over
And it is utterly silent
It is the ultimate silent treatment.
Her boyfriend dumps her
And severs all connections
With her on social media
And the Internet.
He unfriends her on Facebook,
Stops following her on Twitter
And avoids responding to her calls,
Texts and emails.
He just disappears;
Fades out of her life mysteriously
I do not know if she knows
why have emotions fizzled out so soon
Whether she ever thought
Where her love has vanished?
At any moment

She is preoccupied
Or whispers a name other that of her own .
Hasn't she taken her love for granted
As she walked along the love paths of this digital world?
I do not know but I do know now
Making love in the time of apps
In the digital age
a difficult space to negotiate.
It is nothing short of running the most puzzling maze
And turns are getting more twisted than ever before
People are getting unnecessarily hurt.
Look! She is running here,
running there,
Gripping her hands on her heart
Writhing and whirling
To get out of the present pain
While the rich clouds about her curl
Snow falls on the garden.
Upset, repenting

Heaving her white breast to the freezing wind
Torturing grief hangs her head.
Hardly able to stop
Stomping with speed,
Breaks the new snow in her garden
With her wild feet
not tired
And with pain that shall not part,
Until the wet snow is written over
The long sentence
Expressing her pain
Betrayal of her love
In this digital world.
What a way to express the anguish of the soul!

## 14

# Grand Canyon

Seeking and striving for happiness,
I had gone from place to place,
From the Golden Gate,
The Statue of Liberty,
To the bays of oceans,
And valleys of vineyards,
Through wilderness and wide plains,
Mountains and the water fronts,
Discovering the unknown world, like a traveller.
Suddenly I glanced at the awe-inspiring gorge.
Stretching for miles
Descending thousand miles
To the river rapids-
Colorado River.

The Grand Canyon,
On the spring afternoon
Coming out of darkness
And moving into light
Changing and challenging shapes
Manifesting its ever changing
Display of rainbow colours
And endless forms
Opening out
A vast expanse of eternity before me.

Its beauty crowds me.
It speaks of Thee, Thy purity,
Who carves the spaces with deepest colours?
Playing with dark and light,
Presence and absence
Felt insignificant in the presence of this phenomenon.
The physical senses shattered,
Storms of discord and despair,
Winds of pain silenced,
Magic colours send vibrations

Of melting notes into the still depths of the soul,
Lightens up the darkest corridors
Of my being.
The wordless melody echoes in me
Sings the tunes without words
And never stops at all.

Know not the source of this light
But see what it reveals.
Bereft I was,
I saw not this undiscovered continent
Even in my dreams
As a blind beggar feels the warmth of the sun,
The miraculous tunes possess
The secret knowledge of the Ultimate
Carrying the burden of Truth,
Await me, in all things.
It speaks to me of thee
I hear the voice of truth in the silence.
Let it be the sight of thee
Greet the traveller like me.
Let the soul seek meaning.
Content with the slow,
Serene movement of the vista

In the slant of light
I pass the fields of setting sun.
With the vision of the changing,
Shifting world,
The music of the silence echoes in my being

Not stilled even by the chilly fears of unknown.

## Growing old gracefully

Who does not want to live long?
I long to be eighty
Even if my back is doubly bent,
And my shirt hangs on my shoulder
And pantaloons loose
Slipping on the waist
Like a feeble hold on life.

I do not want to find myself
Sighing and frightened.
One can only live
 If one is intoxicated with life.
All I want is to be a cherry old man
Who takes childlike delight?
In finding something in his garden.
Picking his own berries
In harsh summer
Or carrying home apples
In gusty autumn evening
Stopping by to talk to people
In unself-conscious manner.
Being too happy in their happiness
Enjoying the evening of life,
Picking bird like his living
Truly I know the greatest gift
Of old age is its cheeriness.
It is more than thousand sacraments,
Better than the prayer
 Only I am learning to live
Without any apologies for my existence
It is an art one learns while living
Hours upon hours
Of deliberate practice.

## Happiness

Like everyone else
I started to build the house of happiness
With money, power and passion.
I planned my life,
Worked hard towards career goals,
Putting money aside in retirement plans,
Sometimes repairing ancestral home,
Sometime constructing my own,
Adorning it with romantic love
Pleasures of raising children
Music of their pranks and progress,
Their rising career graph and status
Spending most of the hours,
Of most of my days
Constructing tomorrows
I hope will make them happy
I toiled and sweated to give them
Whatever was crucial for their wellbeing
Squirreling away portions of pay checks
Each month so that they can enjoy
The world they inherit from me
With the grandchildren bouncing on their laps

Always priding on my struggles,
And self-sacrifices.
Inevitably assuming it stood solid.

Life was swift, I was fifty and asked
Have I arrived at the final destination?

Mistaken as I was in my view,
Ripples taken for a sea.
Then a strange thing happened
When by accident knocked on the ground
I stumbled on life,
That folded me in its warm embrace

Showing me:
Happiness is the ever-changing foam
That floats on the surface of life.
Joy and pain,
Like the two separated shores,
Mingle their voices in a song of unfathomed life.
Everything changes and moves:
This movement is life.
Life is everything.
It said pretty simple: get a real life
Savour its varied tastes in sufferings and joys
There is no condition
In which I need be unhappy and not free.

Oh! I was looking for it every where
When it lay so close to me
It was within me
It was not the destination
It was the partner of my journey

Afterwards movement of life went on
Ceaselessly as the flow of time
Compressing it, sometime destroying it,
But always rotating on the same essence.

## Higher consciousness

O Lord,
Will a man one day raise his consciousness?
As high as Fuji Mountain,
Stand really tall
To experience the world
From higher dimension
Across the void,
Across the Universe
And measure out with God's image.

Would he not ever move?
Beyond himself,
His survival,
His cravings,
His self-interest,
His self-justifying outlook,
His own success,
To enlarge the human spirit
Loosen his hold on his own ego,
Cast off
A little of the customary self-justification,
Brittle pride.

And ascend to a less biased
And more universal perspective,
To be unmoored from the baggage
Of spiritualism
And superstition
To enrich his understanding
What it means to be human.
To understand that people's behaviour
Is driven by pressures.
Their temper or viciousness,
Are symptoms of hurt rather than "evil"?
Rather than explaining their actions
Only in terms of how they affect us.

To awaken him:
The appropriate response
To humanity is not fear,
Cynicism or aggression,
But always — love.

And when God comes down
To measure man
He finds him good.
Let not the hours pass by
Oh Lord,
Will your take his hand in your hand?
And lift him
Like you lifted the Goverdhan Parbat
On your little finger,
And to reveal the world _
Notonly a place of suffering
And ceaseless effort,
But also a place of tenderness and longing,
Beauty andtouching vulnerability.

## Hot springs of Tattapani

Showing me, the vast expanse of water
A child said, where are the hot springs?
How could I answer the child?
I do not know where they are anymore than he.

Hot springs
-The miracle of the nature -
Visible on the banks
Of deep and cold waters of Sutlej in Tattapani
A sulphur-scented gift,
Designedly bestowed
Bearing the creator's name
Reminding the onlookers,
Somewhere in the corners of hearts,
To see and say
Oh My Lord!
Now swallowed
By the backwaters of Kol Dam
Built at Slappar.
I looked for the solid, old bridge
Britishers made long ago,
Various old huts of the villagers
That lined up the slates paved road to the springs
They too got the watery grave I guess
I see no trace of Vishnu temple,
No branches of the old Peepul tree
Laden with the red threads,
The devotees hung
To remind the reigning deity,
To grant their wishes.
What has become of the young and old men?
What has become of the women and children
Who lived in those houses?
Near the submerged bridge
Only few roofless walls
With broken windows

And shattered slates
Are still visible on the higher hill,
To tell the sad tale of
The uprooted,
The ousted.
There is no trace of the Sarai
Where travellers sought the shelter
And reston their onward journey to Manikaran.
Now the water is murky, dark with the silt.
It is neither lake nor the sprawling open pond.
Just an expanse of water above
River Sutlej under it
Hiding in shame
The handiwork of man
In the name of development.
No newcomer will know
What happy people lived here?
Content with what little yield
Their small land gave.
No grandfather could show with pride
His child where his roots lay.
Only like me can point out to somewhere,
In this still murky water.
Are they alive and well somewhere
 Who will come to tell?
How are they
Dealing with the loss of something familiar.

Moving away from something one knows
Toward something one doesn't
Is a universal stressor
To nearly all species,
Their breath roaring out, to unfamiliar sky
All alone,
Without hope,
Without life and neighbourhood
Poor flesh, sad bone.
They tear, they bleed,
They scar.
They tell no one
They are ousters.
That is just the way it is.

# How do we know what we want?

Who does not love life?
Who doesn't want to live well?
Why is it then
All including philosophers are utterly baffled
As to how to proceed,
What should be done?
And how it might be lived
Even though we may've lived a dozen in the past
Of which we remember nothing.
How hard we might try to recall life
We cannot remember anymore
The time when we were not here
Not born yet.
There is no way of knowing.
What life will be or will not be
After we died.

We have only one life
And we only live once,
No rehearsal or reprise.
We can neither compare it
With our previous lives
Nor perfect it in our lives to come.
This ill prepares us for living.
How do I live you?
Oh, this way and that way.
Oh, happily, perhaps
Yes I have no axis,
No previous experiences,
Nor any ideas
Of the present script.
I know not even my calling.
My life is a sketch for nothing,
An outline with no picture.
Never in my life have I felt so empty.

There is no means of testing
Which decision is better?
There is no basis for comparison.
Even the right choice presents itself
Shrouded in uncertainty and doubt.
We live everything as it comes, without warning

Is life a process of dealing with not-knowing?
There is not one
Who says, "I chose my life "
Rather we are chosen
by something invisible, powerful,
Uncontrollable and beautiful.

# Lord of my life

If this be, Thy play,
then take this fleeting emptiness of mine.
Why is it that birds should sing?
So beautifully and bring joy to whole family,
Beautifully end as a heap of feathers.
If your loving touch is on their limbs,
It is on mine too.
I also want to love this life
This is the last chance
I'm ever going to get to be alive.
And knowing Thy powers alone
Can give me strength
To complete the picture
You have outlined of my life,
To fill it with watery and earthly colours,
Suitable to thy fiery designs
Within Thy frame of Time and Space.
My anguished soul cries out
For thy healing touch:
"O serene
 Free
In thy immeasurable mercy,
Wipe away these dark stains from my heart.
Kindle the light in the darkness of my being
To illuminate me from within
To sail through the river of life.

## I am not a saint

There are days when all I want
Is to be free of her
And her neediness.
I am nothing like a saint
She wants to make me out.
I resent her for being the way she is.
I resent her for the narrowed borders of my existence,
For being the reason
My best years of ease
 And pleasures are flown.
Now I understand
Why old sages went so deep in the forest
Or into the high mountains
Or miles away to holy Ganga Ghats
To lose into the mist or wave.
One day I also set out
Along with the long list
Of what all I would do
Where I would go.
Wherever I went ,
Her world came after
I could still see
Her blue veined hands
Wrinkled face
And pleading eyes
My stares were open and apologetic
I tried to conceal my screams
But murmured :
I am not a saint
But accept the great task
Of carrying life forward .

## I ask myself

I ask myself why I suffer
From a false and distorted sense of my own existence
Why my ego,
Enclosed in a bag of skin
Keeps me separate from the universe?
Why I resist change
And long for immortality in an impermanent universe.
Why it gets intolerably inconvenient to accept:
"All is change, all is flux."
Why I cling to the notion of the self,
Despite it's ever -changing essence?
Why the fleeting nature of things so disturbs me?
Why I cling to the old things?
Why I visit and revisit the old neighbourhood where I grew up,
Searching for the remembered grove of mango trees
Near the Sutlej river,
Why I clutch my old photographs.
Why I pray to the everlasting and eternal.
While in every nook and corner,
Nature screams at the top of her lungs
That nothing lasts, that it is all passing away.
All that I see around,
Including our own bodies,
Shifting and evaporating.
With age, muscles slacken,
Grow loose,
Lose mass and strength
In a few short years,
Will be gone.
My atoms will be scattered in wind and soil,
My mind and thoughts gone,
My pleasures and joys vanished,
My "I-ness" dissolved in nothingness:
Muscle to flab
Vigour to decrepitude
Breath to air

Dust to dust.
Why the notion of all that has been
And no longer is
Feels unbearable.
Then why strive for youth and immortality
Is it that I am being emotional and vain?
In my wish for eternal life
Is it that it exists beyond time and space?
Outside nature.
Is it I am delusional, or nature is incomplete.
Will anyone tell me what is it?
Despite my struggle and howl
Against the brief flash of this life,
It's beauty and grandeur fascinate me
Take me beyond sorrow,
Careless and walking on the air.

Tell me what else beauty could be for
If not to hold one in clear clasp of joy
Not through weaponry of reason
But of pure submission.
I am happy to be alive in this world
Might be one summer
This mortality,
Like that night-blooming cereus,
Opens to reveal silky white petals,
Delicate and fleeting as life in the universe.

## I awoke before the sunrise

I awoke before the sunrise
Peered through a frosty window,
A scene dim and vague
With flowing mists.
The sun is not yet in sight
Signs of its advent are plain to see.
Pale purple clouds sail
Like a fleet of ships
Across the golden dawn.
The last fogbanks
Are scudding away like ghosts
Before the wind and the sunrise.
Morning sky is bright blue
And sun mellow
Animating presence of the land
In the morning glory.

Over and over,
I surrender to the land's rhythms,
Its fragrances and its sweetness,
The mighty stillness embraces.
Instead of loneliness I feel loveliness.
I feel a quiet exultation
Looking at
Over there, natural arches,
Holes in the rock,
Windows in stone,
Huge sandstone walls,
The pure sun shinning on all.

What else can you do?
When mysteries present themselves,
You mistake this grandeur for godliness.
Is not this the work of a cosmic hand?
Images of rainwater,
Melting snow,

Frost and ice
Come to mind doing its work quietly.
I, gaping at this spectacle
Of rock and cloud
And sky and space,
Spider, squirrel circling around pine trees
Possessing all I admire in them.
I want to meet creator
Face to face,
Even if it means risking
 Everything human in myself

I dream of merging with a nonhuman world.
I feel a ridiculous greed
And possessiveness come over me.
I want to know it all,
Possess it all,
Embrace the entire scene intimately,
Deeply, totally,
With no one, human, non-human
To dispute possession with me.
It is love too fierce to endure,
I opened the door and ran to it
Like insane.

# I never thought her memories would hurt her

I never thought her memories would hurt her.
Her world was warm, sparkling like April sun.
She was strong, unyielding to pain or suffering
Her soul ever filled with joy.
I thought nothing could hurt her.

And suddenly her world turned gray,
Darkness wiped her joy away,
As she turned ninety four
With solemn eyes.
Her vivid memories twirl
Like coloured tops through time
Nor stop to understand
Her mami whose death she mourns now
Had died long ago.

Loud, still, louder she cries
Love flames forever if the flesh be grieving.
Memories came as things come that will perish,
Or to be seen or heard awhile in the middle of sleep
Or came again at the moment of waking.
Sometime small or remote,
In the morning
All shall bet he same again:
Her own mind turns traitor,
Plots with her old saggy body
Hauls them round with it again
Like merry-go-round.
She is caught
In the web of mortal losses.

How she is still burning to death
Within her own gloomy hell.

Unaware, mom never will learn:
How all their play is touch-and-go?

But, I cry.
Eye breaks a tear
For each quick, flaring game of her mind
As that of child, leaf and cloud.
Her stonier eyes,
Fixed in their rocky sockets
Chill me to death.
Now there is nowhere I can go
To hide from her:
Even moon and sun reflect her pain .

## After the break-up
## I ran to the woods

I didn't make rows,
I did not say all sort of unpleasant things
That mentally tears you to pieces.
Though most difficult sacrifice of all is giving away
The very thing you want to hold forever.
I kept walking with my exquisite pain,
Reached the thick woods
I hugged the tree.
It asked with the eyes of silence more than with the lips.

Is it not strange that you utter the first thing
That has been bothering you
When you find a patient listener in the other?
I also blurted out:
Unconditional love does not seem to exist anymore
In the world in which I am born.
No one sits gazing,
Sighing, saying sweet nothings :
I am in love with you
I did not sleep, I wrote verses
I love you more than myself,
More than anything in the world.

Instead he sat looking at me
Neither horribly awkward,
Nor unbearably miserable,
Nor heavy hearts or embarrassed eyes,
No agonizing, strange soul revolting silence.
Straight he said
I am not deceiving you
Nor concealing from you.
Love is not crime,
No will can struggle against it
You are free to give yourself happiness.

After all I am not the first and won't be the last.
Perfect freedom, they say,
Is an essential condition of love?
Love cannot bear anything vague or indefinite
And he left me in a jiffy.
How happy are these
Who can take a load off their conscience like that?

If love returned resembles not the love given
It is difficult to forgo the disappointment that flow.
To struggle against this love is beyond my power

You have told me your despair
I will tell you mine, the tree said
Have you ever seen stripped and bare woods?
Their leaves and flowers once beautiful,
Then their petals blown and withered rot,
On the earth that gave birth to them all.
Have you ever heard any tree
Lamenting the loss of season and its passions?
Why to the heart of man
Is so difficult to go with the drift of things,
Bow and accept the end of love
As the end of the season.
I listened in silence and returned home
There after no more attempts at
Vulnerability, powerlessness, exquisite pain
To which go apprentice in any relationship.

# If God comes

If God comes
How shall I greet him?
Shall I not dread him?
Shall I not fear him?
After such a long period of waiting?
Though I have cried for him

All these years I have prayed
I haven't forgotten my little presentiment:
My life be over before He got to me.

If sun rises
I have a word with God
Life would not be the same.
What if I wake one cool morning?
To hear the hammering
Of His soft hands on my hard wooden door.
Should I suffer the trembling of my weak legs?
Or ostrich to my dark room
To hide in cozy, familiar darkness
To let the sleep hang
Heavily on my dark droopy eyes

Or is he just a beautiful, exotic dream?
If he is
I do not want to wake up
Sweet is the familiar,
Sweet is snug complacency,
Sweet is sleep of unawareness.

## Innocence of a child

It is the moonlit night of March,
Rays reflecting in the rippling lake,
The sweet smell of jasmine is in the air,
What do you say, Kuhu,
Of sitting out on the balcony
And watch the moon rise.

It is Purnima tonight.
It is full moon
Wrapped in starry light.
She lies on soft blue bedspread of sky
While south wind caresses
Her cloudy, glittery hair
And seems to lead her in dance
With its sweet colours and sounds.
Her pure, glowing face,
Her starry veil thrills my heart
It makes me dance like crazy
And rejoice beneath the starry sky
Her solitary image in my heart
Every time pulls me
Into its vortex of unrelenting self -finding:
Makes me think about mystery
Beyond the present time and space.

I want to forget
Wiseman's warning:
Life is but a dewdrop on the lotus leaf.
I neglect all this to gaze
This perfect beauty
Revealing, withholding and screening again .
Oh! How enriching
To love this world!
Like a great love,
It makes me feel
Closer to my inner being,

Envelops me'
In its immutable and caring magic
It also beckons me
With its steadfast and singular mesmerism.

Meanwhile,
Fresh face of Kuhu peeps across
With her raised eyes to my eyes.
She looks at me
Not in carefree or serious way
Not in the way you love
Or in the way you praise
But in the way you are happy.
Staring off into space
Like when you were a kid,
Stray out of all words
Into the ever silent.

# 28

# It happens once

This course is offered only once
Even if I come here improvised
And leave without practice.
Even if I know nothing of the script,
It is handed over on the spot
I cannot rehearse it
Nor can I repeat the words
Impulses and acts of yesterday.

It is always new
It is my role
I cannot exchange it
I have to perform it
There is no time to show strange fright
Or express ignorance
Or say asides or soliloquies.
The stage is set
Heavens are watching,
Record keeper is busy
All my actions are for ever
When I leave the stage
They will be carried forward to the next.

# The lord loves you

It was many many years ago
I was a child by the side of the sea
The moonlight from the silent bough
Suddenly with precision spoke my name.
A wind blew from the cloud
In the night breathed: the lord loves me well.
I felt my bosom swell
Filling me with the joy.
I have wandered home but newly
With this ultimate truth.
It was love more than love can be.
It was stronger by far than the love of others.
Angels in heaven envy me,
The demons down under the sea
Can sever it not from my soul.
The wind grew stronger filling me all the more
Now the moon beams bringing me dreams of you
The stars rise to remind me of your bright eyes
I lie by the noon tides, night tides,
Listening to sounding sea
To reassure me of your love.
And they kiss my pallid brow,
Murmuring lowly, murmuring for ever
I sigh
"Oh, I am happy now!"
I dream I do not know how:
Good lord,
Could I awaken in your vast chamber?
Where you dwell
Surrounded by the seraphs of heaven,
Ministers singing
How will I know you unless I see you
Soaked in your love in this blue sepulture.

## Landscape

In this masterpiece,
Spring has been detained eternally.
My woman has lingered under the pine trees
Whose roots have overgrown
With green blades of grass.
See how far behind she has left me.
A violet hat and crimson skirt she wears
Forever,
Young and happy.
What bliss hides behind her song
Whose notes waft forever on this tree?
Away from the living muddle and mysteries
Human pain and despair
That is really mine.
Even if I call her she would not hear
Even if she hears she would not turn back.
Even if my heart is beating hundred miles an hour
My face would seem a stranger's
Aged, greyed and unrequited.
For what is love
If not the gift of being seen for who one is?

Even if I stand in her way
Stare in her face,
Make grand gestures
To render me worthier of her love
She does not take step closer to me.
She would pass by me finer than a thread.
On her right is my house
She knows it from inside with its doors and stairs.
Her love never sneaks in through the back door
To watch how life goes on unpainted behind.
Nor move out of that frame
To know on which unknown sea
Other passengers of the ship have moved on.

I do not know the games of her heart
But I know she would always hold on
To that landscape
While my universe is in constant flux,
And keeps staring at me
With those inimitable eyes of hers
As the April sun gleams on her,
A flock of birds take flight in the sky.

## Live in - Relationship

All my young age
I have felt
There is something more wonderful
Than marriage or staying single.
I did not know what it is.
But every morning
On the wide lanes of Basant Kunj
I pass by the young couples
Staying in live in-relationship.
How amazing!
Falling in love,
Finding your passion,
Living with him.
No need of parental consent,
No dowry, no ritual,
No strings attached to relationship

One day in spring,
A boy came
In the lovely form of the Lover
To give to my dreams, sweetness.

He came and sat by me.
Taking my hands in his, he said:
"You do not know me, but I do .
The thread of love with which I would bind you
Binds me too.
That I want you only".
His heart repeated without end.

It felt you wanted someone,
You were deprived of something,
And then it seems to be there.
Suddenly a wild wave
Broke over my heart's shores
And drowned all language.
We shared a bond

Of uncommon magnitude and passion,
Were busy building life- bridge forever between us.

Suddenly it snapped and crumbed.
It almost vanished into something else.
He stayed serene,
Didn't feel a thing
Yes, he turned his head away
After he said good bye.
Here is the apartment
But the love has gone by,
Lost to the institution of marriage.
Yes it cuts and wounds while setting you free.

What are you going to do?
What can you do about it?
Live in relationship is like a revolving door
You have an easy entry,
And much easier exit too.

This is not about losing
But about how I rose from the ground
And saw the world as if for second time
The way it really is.
I do not want to sit down at home and cry.
I want to walk in life
Owning my responsibility
That comes with the choice.
Life is an invitation to happiness if done right
I steadied myself
Reached out,
Picked the broken pieces
From the ground around.
For hours in my trembling hands
They glittered like fire.
Is it necessary to say anymore?
As for me I am still alive you see
The battle still rages on,
Life struggles so stubbornly,
Determined to keep living even when he is gone.

# Losing someone

Anyone who has ever lost the loved one
Knows how anguishing,
How painful it is!
A paralyzing fear grips you
When you think of losing someone you love.
It metastases into all-consuming grief
When one does lose.

Nothing prepares you for the death
Knowing he would die did not prepare me.
After all he made it possible for me to live
I feel completely shutting down emotionally,
Dead from inside
It is like waking up in the world that has lost the sky.
I feel loneliness
But the sense of being lost takes me unaware.

But it comes slowly.
First sensations of distress,
Then tightness of throat,
Shortness of breath, choking,
An empty feeling in the stomach,
Lack of strength,
Finally intense pain of loss.

My longing for the lost time is acute.
I remember the things
I think I have forgotten,
Memories, seemingly so trivial,
Consume me.
I am seeking him,
In landscape of my life,
In the objects and animals around me,
But he, absent and hiding.
My voice does not reach him.
It seems his eyes have flown away.

Death has sealed his mouth
He is distant and silent like stars
All things are filled with his soul
He emerges from all things.

Embodied presence of the loss
Becomes the physical part of life.
Everything like a little boat
Carries me to him
It is like a snow storm,
Like snow falling to the ground
My inner experience bleeding into it.

I am saying but not believing he is dead
I can neither absorb it
Nor move forward as everyone advises.
I throw myself in work
Or mourn in the privacy of inner life
Alone, away from public eye,
The unspoken rule in any culture,
Even then I cannot muscle through pain.

Many people believe:
Sensible and rational women
Can keep it under control
With the strength of will and character.
I seem to lack both.
Modernity has left me bereft of rituals.

How I wish I could cry
Like soldiers in The Iliad with Achilles
On the fall of Patroclus
I am not an emotional warrior either
It is not a question of getting over either,
Or healing up.
It is a question of learning to live with the transformation.
Loss is transformative.
A tangle of change
What I had of that soul in a bag of skin
Is a small pouch of ashes in my hands?
That is enough matter
That would go to the ground

And mix with new organic matter
But there is solace of new existence
Suffused with joy
I feel my eyes traveling
Beyond the bright treescape.

There are many worlds
Beyond my perception
My partner is indelibly there.
I put my hand on the gate
World goes ablaze.
I stand there
With a kind of peace
Humming in my blood.
I feel like playing in the drama,
Script of which had all been written-
That I don't want to understand or need to do
What I would do,
How I will live,
Already known.

# Love her

I always shoo her away like a cur-
Unwanted and disturbing -
Many a time
I say 'oh you! Just Go.
Run like the devil,
Try not to find me.'
She turns away in despair.
Again she comes
Working her way towards me
Calling where I am perched
Warning 'you cannot do this.'
She tries to mesmerize me,
Wooing with words and persuasions.
They are all in vain.
I cannot hear,
All her lowing, shouting, counselling,
I keeping none.
I never lamented once
Carried not an ounce
Of emotional weight or guilt.

Still she enters unbidden
As one of the crowd
Unknown and uninvited,
Trying to reign my thoughts
Actions and dreams,
Press her signature on
My trivial conflicting moments of life.

I keep her alone and apart
While I roam from country to country,
Careering through life,
Keeping it in my capable hands
That I won't feel her lift and lag
Throughout the journey .

Growth and decay of my life rose and fell
It was evening before I came to feel
What I was hearing and missing.
It was when I lighted my candle
and went up to my room that night
All of a sudden
There appeared to me a stranger.

Had I not been awake
I would have missed it again.
And by chance I sighted
Her in my mirror
In my own house
And could recognize:
She was my roommate
Who lived with me for years
But like body and soul apart.

Now face to face is an experience,
Everything and nothing spoken
Still intimate and helpful
Like a cure you did not notice happening.

Our eye beams threaded laser fast
No transport ever like it.
Her eyes leave not mine
Giving us time to look together
And away from our parting.
I know the pain of loss
Her sight has the power-
The power I feel came up through
And earths me here for real.
And smile at the stranger -
Who is my self -
Who has always known me
Like a local road,
Every turn of it in the past,
Has loved me all my life
Whom I have ignored.
Who cares for me?
Now she appears to me

Open, mendacious and illumined
And I, radio without battery.

Time has arrived to welcome her -
Make her sit at my table,
Treat her
Feast on
To celebrate her arrival.

# Morning mountains range beyond Simla town

There is a luminous glow.
 Is it you coming
Silent footed with the rays of the sun?
Is it really you?
Rising out of the foam of the waves
Stroking the mouth of the oceans on the sides of shore?
Is it you behind those deodar trees beyond my courtyard?

In the scented night lit by the galaxy of stars
Trees, the rivers and mountains change for a while.
The wind draws the shadow of clouds around the moon.
Your immense body cast a shadow on my eyes,
I could feel a kiss on my cold hands.
Is it you or the kind wind whispering in my ears?
Yeah ,yeah .

I could feel your scented breathing
In the distant breath of the rain.
I could feel the force lifting me-
Captive of flesh,
Towards you.
Is it the way you show your love?

I cannot explain my happiness
And the way it erased all signs of sorrow.
I could not see you there,
Being no moon
And the stars sparse.
I heard you in the rain dripping on the porch.
In the wind rustling the leaves like papers,
In the solitude of soundless things.
I do not know what is happening in my heart.
There is nothing like your Beauty –
In the falling of the leaves

In the night that is dark.
In the sky that is great
In the heart
That is murmuring of innermost dancing.
In silence
The heart raves.
It utters words
Meaningless
Thickens my blood
I thought I would die if I see you
How could I exist in the same world with that brightness?
Why would someone show these shadows of truth
Unless He is there.
Is not it the way you show your love?

## Michigan River

I sat looking out of the open window
Of Millennium Apartments in Chicago
To the brilliantly lit Michigan River.
Full many an hour did I spend
In the strife of the empty days
To draw my heart on to it.
When sad birds twitter ceaselessly,
 Summoning lost companions
I am sunk in lonely pensiveness.
Tear-soaked memories sway me,
Stir my mind to the Himalayas,
Their icy peaks
Coolly gleaming in the starlight,
Casting my home ,
Its courtyard
In ethereal silver.

How the moon transforms
A familiar scene into something quite magical!
An orange square of light
 Flicks to life.
 A cool breeze stirs,
Bringing with it ribbons of night jasmine
Along with curiously beguiling new scent
Carried on the breeze.
It is a familiar fragrance,
Reminding something of the magic moments:
My world was warm with April Sun
My thoughts spangled green and gold
My soul filled with joy.

Suddenly this coming to Chicago eclipsed my world,
It turned grey,
Darkness wiped my joy.
Now I feel the sharp pain,
The estrangement

A dull and aching void.
Careless hands destroyed
My silver web of happiness.
How frail the human heart is!

Now I see white boats with blue masts
Floating on the surface of the Michigan river,
Bridges, viaducts, waterways
The Navy Pier, the Museum, the glass observatory
Flanking its banks.

I lift my face to the wind,
The gulls swooping breathlessly so high overhead
Seem to brush their whirring wings
Against the blue roof of the sky.

Who can understand another!

'Everybody should be little quiet
by the river and listen' they say
Its silence invites
To pay selfless and unselfconscious attention
to the world.

The river is creating,
Nourishing,
Opening up new areas
and objects of attention.
Purged by silence,
I am also able to pay attention
To everything around.

Suddenly I could hear the river
Saying lovingly:
I have also left my source
But nourished the places along its shores
On my way to meet up with the ocean.
At that moment,
The brown and grey plumaged sparrow
With a baby or baby's baby
Alighted gently
Over the silent bosom of the river

Spreading its broad wings
Folded against its body
In golden hues
Pure and bright delight.

Seeing what I have seen
Has filled me with hope
May be some day
My child or my child's child,
Holding his hand
Will be standing here,
Hot with the joy of the world
Filled with the praise,
Entire world preserved
And cherished in his chest
Like a precious jewel in a necklace.
And me free from the servile bondage to the world
And deliverance from time.

## My other self

You can never go home again
I have married
Got children,
Have grown up.
No, rather I have grown old,
I have accumulated years
In my body and in my face.
Arriving at home I looked up
in the mirror at the door
It said hello to the stranger
Which was my real self
I searched shadows,
Fears ,dreams ,dragons
Hiding under the skin,
In the extreme corners of the eyes
Or in the gristle of ear lobe.

Where is it -
The real self?
Has it melted in my grasp
Or fled before I touched it
Or gone in the act of becoming
Or has time – the unforgiving dictator of life
wrapped it up?
Oh! No
It had always been with me
when the road was tough,
Getting tougher
And others shouting me down
"correct your course",
Its voice kept me company.
Peel it off the mirror
Sit, celebrate life
Or Time speeds up as we grow old.

## New castle

Everyone says
Ocean is calm, blue and placid.
I went to New castle
Found it pure, powerful and playful.
The lake Macquarie comes
Circling around many towns for miles
To meet it on New castle.
It raises its arms of sand dunes
Folds its vast waters
In an embrace of pure joy
White and sacred.
It dances with abandon,
Waves rising high
Making frothy white roars
Surfers bubbling
Up and down
Along with its rhythmical movements,
Feeling its might under its watery feet
Forgetting all the existential dissatisfaction within.
I could not help
But be happy in such a happy company.
For a moment forgot
In few years you would vanish
the ocean will be here
Flowing forever
With its dark blue colour
Its white masts
New onlookers marvelling
At its immensity,
Its new playfulness.

# Night

Why don't you come with me
To the Bondai beach at night
To gaze the reigning queen of darkness,
The night.
 It's vast serenity,
The mystery of its infinite space,
The austerity of the stars,
 Each one of them pouring forth its soul in sheer ecstasy.

Do not be afraid
They are intimate
They turn their faces towards you
To tell you stories:
How the city lights trouble them,
How thick fog
Blocking the view of the night
Makes it unseen and unseeable in the pitch dark.
How the day takes long
To abandon the sky.
Sometimes they take you,
With the other companions of darkness:
The silence and the solitude,
Sailing into the islands of stars,
Voyaging across the horizons
Of sea, of space and time.

Night is beautiful at the beach
No lights stab it without meaning,
Clouds float in the heavens,
In the splendour of space and stars.
The Milky Way bridges the earth and ocean.
I am standing on the beach,
With surf breaking at my feet,
I can see the endless tides rising,
Withdrawing,
The ocean's white froth.

The great earth rolling up
The deeps of heaven and universe.
A new door opening to the human spirit
To another place and another time.
And mystery of being touched
At the glimpse of ourselves,
Our world in the stream of stars.

Every night I see something
That kills me with delight,
It is holiness, it is beauty, and it is eternity.
It is so enchanting.
My heart tickles a doubt
Whether it is within me
To ask these stars,
With Snow White eyes
To lend me a little of their light
To dispel the darkness of my being
And to keep and hold the rapture
of being here tonight.

# Oh lord I know one thing

Oh Lord I know one thing:
When I look at the white moon,
 At the red branch, dry leaves
Wrinkled body of trees in autumn
Or when flowers open their hearts
-Bottles of perfume -
Petals fall
At my window.
Everything ,
These sights, scents, sounds of spattering rain,
Moist half open leaves
Carry me to you,
As if everything that exists,
Were little boats
That sail toward you.
These forms, colours, drifting fragrances
Are the ways you love me.
In your infinity
My life and its dreams live.
Each day,
Each hour,
I want to feel your implacable sweetness,
With each honeysuckle
That climbs up my window sill
And takes me in the net of your beauty
As vast as the sky.
My lord, you come to me
Like the fresh breath
That passes through my life.
Do not stop loving me
 My life survives on your love.

If suddenly you would forget me
Do not look for me,
And leave me at the shore of my heart

Even on that day,
at that hour,
I shall lift my arms
Clasp my hands in prayer to seek you
And shout to the afternoon winds
You are mine.
Ah my love, ah my lord
I cannot survive except
Being in the fold of your arms
As long as I live.
And drown in the final wave of your love and life.

# Old people's home

Here comes Eliza with her lipstick and red bindi
Her hero's memories deep in her mind.
He exists exactly as he did inside her motherly womb.
She says looking towards heaven:
I would not have been here
If he was not killed in Kargil war .
She keeps asking me:
Why there is no visit from your sons
Even though they were not killed.
As if they do not owe it to me.
"If my son has lived through the war
Sure I would be spending my summer
With him in Srinagar.
He would have sent the uniformed chauffeur
To take me home
To show all of us
How much he cares for his old mother".
What makes her so sure?
She keeps on singing the old song
While all old home folks smile at her back
She seems to forget her son's gone
It is too late to understand the changing times.

# 41

# One needs a teller

One need a teller
To make you realize the glory of knowing;
Who you are and what you are.
One wants a teller
Even if you are a grown up man or a woman
 In modern times of aggressive haste
To bear enormous burden all alone in this productive world.

He tells you which nobody else in the world can tell:
What it is like to be alive.
And all you have ever wanted to do.
He will not solve your problems,
But to outline what the problems are.
And to stretch, to shake up, to overreach yourself,
Go into yourself,
Find a way of living with otherness
In order to live with yourself.

One is not certain if or why or how.
One wants a Teller:
Here's hell, there's heaven.
Be cool, time brings all good things-
And becalms our momentary tumults
Against the raging brain
That washes the shoreline of the human spirit.
Look
Love's true, and triumphs;
And God's there.

# At the Pond's lake

Every morning I walk swiftly
With forward glances to the Pond's lake.
The waters have settled after the night of rain.
I do not dip the cupped hands in the lake
I feel cold in body
Though the sun is moving along the landscape,
The billowing trees ,thick with blossoms
Glistening.
The centipedes emerging from wet earth
Shaking in the wind,
The pathways circle around the shining lake.
The black ducks float on cold water,
A strange bird fluttered alone in the sky.
A duck swimming in the sunlight saw it.
In the meantime another took a vertical flight
Whistling something sweet
Of connectedness,
Of recognition that we share the same land.
Isn't it beautiful, it said?
True, such moments of silences and stillness
Amplify the existential kinship.
At once I feel one in the family of things
No stranger or visitor anymore.

## Walk on snowy evening

I was walking too fast
I was too far away
I knew what habitually I missed
But did not break my busy gait
On hamster wheel of goal chasing.
This is something we all do,
At varying degrees
At various times
As we settle in safe trajectory of life.
When I did pause, perhaps, by accident itself,
Something miraculous revealed.
Lo, it was snowing,
These individual snowflakes
 Making the winter landscape
Even more of a marvel.
It felt so good to be there in that snowy evening.
Suddenly the snow was falling like stars
Filling the trees in the darkness.
I wanted to stay still
Neither hurrying nor delaying,
Just holding out hands in the air
To feel it's feathery flaky touch.
I saw people striding,
Strolling, rushing, dashing.
I know not
If they were also thinking of stopping by
But I do know
How this sort of crusade for productivity
Takes you away from this pure presence!
Everything was so pure and bright.
The birds for some unknown place
Had taken a flight
Some hid in the fork of the fallen trees at night
What an absolute delight
Just to be alive
To be happy again.

in new way on this earth!
I am not thinking
Nor waiting for something
-an invisible bridge- to other world
I just do not want to know the unknowable,
The mystery that lie buried
In the layer inside layer of snow.
Sometimes there are these moments
That are better than knowing something.
 You just want to stand where you are
To hold in your hands
The tender glitter falling through the air,
Only to look, to listen and lose
Inside the soft white world
To hear the quieter sounds
That emanate from the depths of your being

## 44

# Stop by my house

Stop by my house
When I call you from where I am.
You don't stand still and look around
You keep on working silently
Filling with snow
The hills and the ground.

The only sound is the sweep of the wind,
Slow fall of flakes.
It is still, it is lonely,
It is cold and pure,
Wondrous!
Stop for a while in my little house
While others are sleeping
On this lonely night.

Why do you lie huddled?
Still like those leaves under the oak tree,
No longer blown here and there.
My heart is aching to seek you.
My little house will feel it strange
If I not wake up in the morning of the New Year
In your presence.
You work the whole night
In the silence and the absence of stars.
Snow hardens upon the early morning street,
Frost carves in window panes
The sun rolls up
Like tint of gold
Snow, something as soft as cheese
Makes all senses freeze.
Mind no longer sharp,
Skims over the surface of things.
The sun sparkles on it far off
I am blinded
But I know it is your reflection

In this blinding, sparkling snow.
I am tired of this consort, reason
It is ever disputing and discontented.
I want to divorce this reason that dissatisfies me,
And watch your silhouettes moving
Under the oak trees
On the hard crust of snow.

Stop by my house
 I want to be betrothed to you
At the altar of this snowy silence,
Drink intoxicating bliss
From the dripping of the icicles from the trees
Stop by my house, my lord.
Let me soar with you
In the skies of inner ineffable freedom.
I have been waiting all night
Your footsteps to fall on my door.
Stop by my house, My Lord.

## Prayer

I want to build in Haridwar
A house with logs of deodar.
I will see the sun rise
Between the mountain ranges,
And spread in the Ganges valley its golden hues.
I will repose under the haven
Of passing clouds
On the banks of Ganges
And its sands
In those everlasting days.
And watch with wonder and attention
The earthen lighted divas on the Ganges
Floating like glow worms on the moonlit waters
Of glimmering Ganges.
The dim light of oil lamps
Slowly sailing the silvery waves.
Devotees throng the Ghats
Saying loudly their chants
Moving the beads on their fingertips
Willingly giving themselves
To the power they perhaps understand.

I don't ride their passion and exuberance
Is it that I do not pray?
I do not know exactly what prayer is.
Isn't it that woods whisper to the ground?
Or is it breeze that makes the silent trees
 Sway and dance?
And is it what I hear in the rumble of the clouds
In the voice of wind
In thunder,
Lightening when it sounds in its full strength?
What is it then that makes you dance
With the dancing waves?
Is it that song that
Suddenly comes out of the heart

When you are sitting silently
And looking at the trees
Or gazing at the stars
Or just be wherever you are
True, authentic and spontaneous
Joyful or silent.

I know
I have almost nothing to offer.
But on the edge of the field
I am attentive
I am listening
Don't I wait restlessly the whole day
To have the last glimpse
Of the setting sun
Melting into orange in the sea
And dance on the empty stage before the curtain falls.

# 46

## Sanctum sanctorum

There is no need to crawl on your knees
To reach the shrine on the hill top,
Or slaughter a goat
Smash a coconut
Or bathe God in milk
Wash His feet
Lay before Him offering
Your mind, body and all you have
Or sit like saint in the silence of meditation
Or search a place of worship
When you have a house of God in you
Lord is a guest within you.

There are seven gates
While entry to the inner shrine
Sanctum Sanctorum
Is through the heart alone.

Purify it,
Cleanse it,
Make it shine brilliant like sun.
Expand it
To take your delight in loving all,
As we have one sap, one root.
You will never find the forest
If you ignore the tree
you will never find God
If you ignore the man.
So serve this god
Whom the ignorant call a man.
Someone shouted loudly
Practice love all day to everybody
And show it in actions
You will realize
You're already in shrine.
I figured we are all one

Just as this earth is one island
In archipelagoes of stars.
He is all, all is in Him.

# Spring has come

Spring has come
Dancing at the centre of life,
And striking the chords of love;
The sky opens,
Laughter passes over the earth.
With spring,
Fine bright days have come too.

Life is not dull,
As the earth is fairer to look upon
It is covered with fresh grass,
Fresh leaves are green upon the trees.
The butterflies spread their sails,
There is a warm breeze
From the sea and the open country,
The air seems to be in love
And faint with happiness.

Nature has sprung into new life,
Put on a new array.
New hopes and new desires
Spring on man too.
When everything in Nature is new and fresh
Why it is hard for man to renew life?

I am looking at the flower beds
And thinking why man is not happy?
Every day is a day of joy
For these butterflies and other insects
Sustained by the touch
Of unforeseen flowers.
 In all seasons, a great joy,
They sit flower upon flower
They only know the rhythm
Of a melody so soft,
They hear and have to hum along.

They exist only in themselves
They are element's function.
Each flower opens its buds
They only take what is there,
And leave faithfully behind
Your earth, your bounty.
Only if man could do this too!

# 48

## The black birds

The wall of mist has just opened up,
Fog has rolled in
Before changing its mind
At the last moment
And rising again
When I opened my eyes there was light,
The sun rising spectacularly across mountains
Air so clear
I could feel my lungs turning pink again.

It is the most perfect day,
Sky as blue as the water.
The black birds have arrived early today.
They are cawing, squeaking, whistling so loudly.
I do not know what they are saying.
May be they are calling
Their fellow crows to come where they are:
We love you and want to share
The blue berries that have ripened early on this tree.
May be they are giving direction
Where to go this monsoon in July.
May be it is their conventional way
To foretell the arrival of the visitor as granny says
May be there is joy in their hearts.
My entire soul cries
Make it stop I can bear it no more.

I say hello black birds,
They turn their many shaded brown necks,
Their shiny, dark brown eyes
To ask philosophically
Without words
You have such good fortune
Why not be happy?
They peck at the ripe berries
With long pointed beaks

With that particular brand of gratitude
That comes with time and travel.
They stopped for a while
Stared at me
Wished me luck and smiled
Then opened their broad, black wings
To take a flight
I picked up the plume
Dropped, out of courtesy,
As return gift:
A happy reminder.

# 49

# The cycle rickshaw puller

Whenever I ask you, mother
Why there are long lines of rickshaws
Along the market
Why do you get cross with me?
Tell me don't you like him
Safely ferrying you to Kali shrine
Every Tuesday
In that narrow seat
Tilted down in front wide open
Except it's plastic canopy .

The metal bars you grab
When another speeding rickshaw's spindly wheel hub
Clashes against ours
While he safely drives you
Through honking cars, trucks,
Buses and swarm of rickshaws.

Doesn't he like a tourist guide
Show me new hotels
Or new places?
When he pedals
He is often off his seat,
His hands straight
And stiff on the handle bars.
Is not it hard for him to go uphill?
He gets off and pushes the rickshaw
with 90 kg of you and me in it
Talking breathlessly
About markets on both sides
But he does not complain.

You never say a word
When Dadu in the upstairs' room
Leaning on his right shoulder
Complains all day long

About his aching shoulder,
You never seem to mind it.

Every time I ask you
Something about rickshaw puller
You say "How troublesome you are!"

He is also old
Lives with his wife and child in slum,
Has no house address
Mama, he tells me,
With pure delight
Rippling through his entire body,
He will make his son go to college
He is working hard for that
For his love he can sacrifice his life.

What you say about him
I do not understand.
Have you forgotten what papa says,
We should treat everyone
Equally and respectfully?

Why do you remain so distant,
Keep your doors so tightly fastened
Even to share with him
A piece of coconut offerings.
You curl up your lip, get edgy
Tell me,
Do not disturb me I am busy
If ever I go to play with him
You call me hundred times
And call me what a naughty boy'!

You scold me,
Send me to play with other children
and not meddle in elders 'affairs.
Even when I say
No more noisy words about him
As is your wish
Why do I still,
Like a small boy in a rage,
Wish to strike at everything in this world
And scream.....?

# The sunsets

Already I am no longer looked at with love.
My daughters and son,
After putting me away in Panchkula home
Are gone from here.
Are you better mother, they never ask
They are somewhat polite
And have no covetous jobs here
Thus have flown the nest.

I am not deceived,
I do not think it is winter as yet
As the sun stays and birds continue to sing.
The sweet flowers are drying and dying down,
The grass is turning brown.

It is a real chill out.
This is no warm house
Though they have fitted it with all my needs.
I store my dreams in cabinets of my mind
And resume on such legs as are left.
In such heart,
I drag out days of my hurt
To their last dregs.

I am cold in this cold house
Their echoes tremulously washing down the dining hall.
I am a woman, sick and suffering
Sweet but irrelevant, not essential.
They would cry out of habit if I die.

I am a woman who hurries through prayers.
The intimations of death mark the walls,
The broken windows and the door.
This is a relief
Some deliverance from grief
Free from loneliness and fidgety emotions

And the rest of things in life that are for lonely women.
Nobody wants to know
Where I was
How I was
Now I am no longer here.
The only sanity is this threshold

Life winks
Only small communion with the master shore.
And I incline my ear to the door:
The relatives are coming
Great dilemma
Whether to let me depart from home
Or to put in mortuary with other lost souls
Hovering invisibly and pushing the dark door.
I am cold in this cold home
And this is everything I have for me.
I must wait till they return from their havens.
Still waiting for them like before
To put me to rest in new shore
With hymn and exceeding sun
And flowers here and flowers there.

## Veiling divinity

When I was child they told me,
Both, the visible and which is not seen
Is alike, are God himself.
But few whom thou deigned
To make you known have seen it.
We can see your creation.
But not the one who has created it.
Are we blinded by this dazzling world?
That we cannot see its creator?
How strange it is
He has concealed the soul in the body
And himself in the soul-
Atman within the Parmatman.
Why are these veils?
Layer of layer of mystery
Within the mystery.

What is this, behind the veil?
Is it something dark or something beautiful?
Can you not reveal?
I am sure it is unique.
When I am quiet at work
I feel it looking
I feel it thinking
I feel it working by its rules

If only you know how the veils are killing my days!
To you they are only transparencies.
But the hours of my life are ticking by
And it is the only one life I will ever have.
Is it impossible for you to let yourself be known
Or are you terrified
If the mystery is exploded
The world will go up in a shriek.
Do you find it entertaining?
Does it pay?
If not, then is there any reason?

Whatever, only let down the veil,
The veil, the veil
Even if it were death
I would quietly take it
I would admire the deep gravity of it
Its timeless eyes.
I would know you were serious
To let me enter the pure and clean,
Like a whiff of spring air
While the universe slips silently from my side.

# 52

# Walk with my grandchild

This Sunday morning
My four year-old granddaughter
Asked me to walk with her in New York.
Showed the loveliest things I've ever seen —
We sampled not only the usual
Tourist attractions like the Statue of Liberty,
Grand Central,
To classic funs capes
The Coney Island's Wonder Wheel
And the walk in Central Park,
She made me watch with nostalgic delight
— The Central Park saxophonist,
The archetypal dog walker,
Williams burg Bridge,
The city's iconic water towers
In Blyton park.
She warmly invited me to pause and marvel
At some of the absurd things we humans do:
Watch people run in place without getting anywhere,
A crowd of yoga doers
Making different postures
On their colourful mats in synch with others.

In the science museum
She regaled me with different sounds
The various instruments produce when struck hard,
In her playfulness with rice
Spread like sand for children to play on.
She opened up to others as her nursery books,
Showing feelings not in fonts or formats
But in friendship that requires team work.
While building the rail tracks,
Multicoloured trains with other children,
She sang in full voice,
Danced and rejoiced
Spontaneously

Accepting this multiplicity of their identity.
She could tie herself
To bonds of belonging
With other human beings
We elders take life time to recognize.
When asked me to do
I gave an evasive answer
 Rather a smile in place of openness.
I who pass the buildings,
The trees, each other and even life itself
Like a sleep walker on side walks
Cut off by I -phone, earbuds or solipsism
Could not help to marvel at her art of seeing.
Her absolute unmixed attention
Presupposes faith and love
Isn't it better than our prayers?
Isn't it a wondrous journey
To the centre of the imaginative,
Immensely insightful
Consciousness of the child,
That yields a profound piece of wisdom.
From that night,
Much better than a good dream,
The happiness began,
Inch by inch
And minute by minute,
To move towards me.

## 53

# Walk the dog in fifth avenue

Energy curls over him like wave
The moment he leaves the door.
He stands in front of multimedia fountain
Which erupts in a play of sound, water and light.

City Centre is an oasis of refinement,
An ancient image:
Jesus seated on the stone,
His head tilted woefully into his hand
-An ancient image
A mixture of piety and humour.
He clings to my arm
I can only imagine
What memories are coursing through his mind.
In market square,
Cafe umbrellas cluster by,
The colourfully painted facades
Of baroque-style townhouses.

Children play in the central fountain
Around a statute of the sword bearing mermaid
Unblinking, his eyes shine as he watches them.

He scatters his love notes around
When he stands by old people
Or some child who is crying
Than someone humming or talking.
Declares him in charge,
And is vigilant.
If someone is playing
With the child when he is around,
Peers into the brown eyes of the strangers
Barks aggressively
When someone approaches the stroller.
This transformation is truly astounding for me
Who knows him to be kind and docile
But you can always learn new things.

I stroll through a tidy Square
Past the Christ church,
Life seems to have moved elsewhere;
Here is a feeling of peace,
Solitude and timelessness.
He becomes a master
At reading my emotional state.
When we walk through dark area
He can smell the adrenaline
My body releases when I am scared.
He hears my breathing pattern change,
Observes my body stiffens
And even smells the subtle pheromones body emits
He suspects I do not like them.
What he sees, smells and knows
Is nothing short of a magic.
He notices my clipped tone of voice,
My posture ,
The agitated way I am walking
Or opening drawers
When I am not speaking.
He wants things to be smooth
He sleeps cuddled next to my bed
hen spouse is out of town.
He stays closer to my leg than normal.

His anxiety spikes
When suitcases are pulled out of loft
Or clothes are spread on bed
Before going on a trip.
His body releases oxytone.
When I make eye contact
He gazes at me lovingly
With unselfconscious joyfulness-
Gateway to pure presence

Isn't it amazing what your dog
Mirrors back, reminds us
Humans as often as he can:
This empathy -
This trait of putting on others' shoes.
To consider others -
From how they feel
To what they might want or need
Is the kinder way to walk about the world.

## 54
# What deodars do for human spirit

One summer evening
I stand in the middle
Of Naldehra Road,
Breathing in and out.
Thousands of deodar trees
Stand stately and shining
On the upper side of the road
And run down towards sprawling Sunni valley.

They never miss a spring without rising and spreading,
 With so many, small green knobs dangling.
Who can tell how lovely in July are these ever green trees?
Why they hold on to their branches
These open flasks
Of lively fragrance -the pine scent.
As the cool, gentle breeze passes through these thousand bodies
of trees
Whistling,
The birds of the forest fill the air with a lovely trilling,
Their orchestral music rises and falls.
And these gorgeous trees nod to each other
And rustle their upturned branches
 In gesture of pure exuberance of joy.
What a movement!
So incredibly beautiful,
 Exultant and stately,
A benediction for the evening
Settling on the distant Sutlej River.

No matter how carefully I watch
The tranquil beauty of the deodars,
Its wildness
Its varied moods
I can never completely enter nor completely know.
They know more than we do
About who, what we are.

And set free a larger truth about life:
The perennial incompleteness of being.

Still
Their beauty holds me tightly
With long upturned green arms,
Keeps calling me.
Why do they sing to my soul?

After a long stare,
Surrendering to its transcendent transport,
Distant brawling of Sutlej River shuts down,
Time slows and extends,
The very elements of the soul shiver.
It is a moment when the doors open;
I feel I am granted access to something nameless,
Something enormous and eternal:
Unexpected sense of deep accord,
A deepened coherence, with the world of others.
There is something like joy
Within many levels of self
That says everything without words.
Entranced, I gaze and gaze at the deodars
That blaze up into music,
Into image,
Into the heart
And mind's knowledge
And ourselves.

# Who am I
## Part-I

When I sit every morning on the hill side,
looking into the shining world,
I am thinking who am I?
Am I the body?
'Yes' the body says quickly
I belong here
I am born here
I am real.
Don't you feel
The feet that walk you everywhere,
The eyes and the listening ears,
The tongue, the marvel of touching.
I know what you think, this is foolishness.
What is that
on my waking up from deep slumber
Confirm my experience of peaceful rest?
When I am sleeping,
It is witnessing what I am dreaming.
In the waking, dreaming
Sleeping or deep sleep states,
Who is always with me.

When I work 9 to 5 in the day
To chase my dreams in big villa
Surrounded by flower beds
And neatly clipped bushes,
Feel not comfortable and serene.
Rather walk away angry, frustrated and sad
Placing the blame on person, job or situation.
When everything turns into something
Terrifying and incomprehensible,
Who is it that tells me
The real problem or pain is perhaps within me?
When on the cross roads

I end up judging
My circumstances against others' outcomes
Who is it that carries the lantern
To throw light on what is right or wrong
And remind me to do
What is right
And asks me
Why don't I live the life I intend to do?

Is this very presenceonly reality?
The sense of 'I am'
Saints and sages confirm,
None can deny this presence.

What stops me
from discovering, understanding and finding myself?
Is Self, such a fluid phenomenon?
Why am I afraid to be alone with myself?
What alienates me from my true self?
Is it world of choices
I have unwittingly agreed to,
Or my convictions, passions,
Deeply held urges and desires
That take me away?
Or the element of fate that is at play?
Or my primal fears
Or is it the blame
 I place on abominable situation
That undermines my resolve to change?
When will I choose the road
Without maps and say yes

# Who am I
# Part-II

Who am I?
My name, my occupation,
My personal history,
The shape or state of my body.
Am I the ideas floating in the mind?
Or can I think of myself
An immortal soul
Or divine soul?

If I am an immortal self and peace is all I want
Then why the deal, the money,
The contract, the loss or threat of loss
Unsettles me.
Why I react to people or situations?
Am I trapped in ego
What I react to in others is also in me
I become aware of ego that I am not.
Who am I?
Consciousness
If not who I think I am
If I already am who I am
Why does it remain unmanifest?
Is knowing me rooted in being.
Nothing I can find about myself is me.
Nothing I know about me is me
At times I confuse knowing about myself with knowing myself
Knowing me is being myself
Being myself is to stop identifying with
What I perceive, experience, think, do or feel
Entire Life unfolds in this constant present
But I confuse this present moment
With what happens
Confuse it with the content
So create illusion of space and time.

"Bloody tyrant time" as Shakespeare says
Kills me
It is a raging river that carries me along
A fire which consumes everything.
Everything is subject to time
There is circumstantial evidence,
The Apple that rotted,
The face you saw in bathroom mirror
Changed with the face you had seen 20 years back in the photo
This is reality of time now.
Time is always in the mind,-
The greatest hindrance to knowing myself.
Time is the horizontal dimension of life,
Surface layer of reality
There is the vertical dimension,
Whatever is?
Whatever happens?
Is it the form present takes?
When I resist that form
I create an impenetrable barrier
That separates me from being who I am
Beyond form,
Separates me from the formless one,
Life.

To the journey of hard work and constant effort?
When the entire soul inwardly cries,

When would I get the strength to say
Make it stop I can bear no more
Just then
There is still somewhere deep within me
An infinitesimally small part faintly murmurs:
Just as you can create your prison
You can set yourself free too.
You do not have forever.
Therefore why wait?
Become a faithful and intimate companion
To that formidable stranger you call your Self.